The Penguin Mo... and diversity of contemporary poetry. Every volume brings together representative selections from the work of three poets now writing, allowing the curious reader and the seasoned lover of poetry to encounter the most exciting voices of our moment.

CLAUDIA RANKINE's collections of poetry are *Nothing in Nature is Private* (1994), *The End of the Alphabet* (1998), *Plot* (2001), *Don't Let Me Be Lonely: An American Lyric* (2004) and *Citizen: An American Lyric* (2014). She is also the author of two plays, including *Provenance of Beauty: A South Bronx Travelogue* (2009), and numerous video collaborations, and is the editor of several anthologies including *The Racial Imaginary: Writers on Race in the Life of the Mind* (2015). Among her numerous awards and honours, Rankine is the recipient of the Bobbitt National Prize for Poetry, the Poets & Writers Jackson Poetry Prize, and fellowships from the Guggenheim Foundation, the Lannan Foundation, the MacArthur Foundation, United States Artists, and the National Endowment of the Arts. She is a Chancellor of the Academy of American Poets and teaches at Yale University as the Frederick Iseman Professor of Poetry. In 2016, she co-founded The Racial Imaginary Institute (TRII). She lives in New Haven, Connecticut.

DENISE RILEY is a critically acclaimed writer of both philosophy and poetry. Her books include *War in the Nursery: Theories of the Child and Mother* (1983); *'Am I That Name?': Feminism and the Category of 'Women' in History* (1988); *The Words of Selves: Identification, Solidarity, Irony* (2000); *The Force of Language* (with Jean-Jacques Lecercle; 2004); *Impersonal Passion: Language as Affect* (2005); and *Time Lived, Without Its Flow* (2012). Her poetry books include *Marxism for Infants* (1977), *Dry Air* (1985), *Mop Mop Georgette* (1993), *Penguin Modern Poets 10* (with Douglas Oliver and Iain Sinclair;

1996), *Selected Poems* (2000) and her latest collection, *Say Something Back* (Picador, 2016). She is currently Professor of the History of Ideas and of Poetry at UEA, and has held posts at universities in Britain, Europe, and America. She lives in London.

MAGGIE NELSON is a poet, critic and the author of several works of non-fiction. Her books are *Jane: A Murder* (2005); *The Red Parts: Autobiography of a Trial* (2007); *Women, the New York School, and Other True Abstractions* (2007); *Bluets* (2009); *The Art of Cruelty: A Reckoning* (2011), a *New York Times* Editor's Choice; *The Argonauts* (2015), which won the National Book Critics Circle Award for Criticism; and the collections *Shiner* (2001), *The Latest Winter* (2003) and *Something Bright, Then Holes* (2007). In 2016, she was awarded a MacArthur 'Genius' Fellowship. She currently lives in Los Angeles.

MODERN POETS 6

Die Deeper into Life

Claudia Rankine

Denise Riley

Maggie Nelson

PENGUIN BOOKS

PENGUIN BOOKS

UK | USA | Canada | Ireland | Australia
India | New Zealand | South Africa

Penguin Books is part of the Penguin Random House group of companies
whose addresses can be found at global.penguinrandomhouse.com

Penguin
Random House
UK

This collection first published 2017
001

Set in Warnock Pro 9.65/12.75 pt
Typeset by Jouve (UK), Milton Keynes
Printed in Great Britain by Clays Ltd, St Ives plc

A CIP catalogue record for this book is available from the British Library

ISBN: 978–0–141–98709–5

www.greenpenguin.co.uk

CONTENTS

CLAUDIA RANKINE

DENISE RILEY

MAGGIE NELSON

Claudia Rankine

New Windows

The stewardess gave me – I had just
turned six – a white eyelet sweater.
It was late November, 1968. 'This is America,'
she told me, 'cold, not like the West Indies.
One needs a jacket of some kind here.'

                    I trailed off.

The white southern businessman needed
to talk. He wanted a story, or more
precisely, he wished to understand how
he came to be sitting next to me in first
class on that otherwise ordinary Thursday.

. . .

This morning when the doorbell rang
and a man stood outside my door,
I thought he must be official,
the doorman has sent him up unannounced.
So I opened my door to him,
smiled and said: *Good morning.*
He was a slender man in his forties,
blue eyes, with a part in his off-blond hair.
He kept both hands in his pants' pockets.
They were gray suit pants. For a minute
he said nothing, giving me time
to accept him as he looked past me
in search of – I'll use his words –

I need to speak to your employer,
to someone who lives here.

. . .

After he left – he had come
about new windows – I remembered
the southern businessman. His litany
of questions. His need to place.
The persistence with which he asked,
You aren't a lawyer, are you?
His curiosity had made me laugh,
so I told him everything,
described everything, including
the first airplane I ever flew in.
The one that brought me here.

. . .

It's been wanting to rain all morning
and without the sun subtracting
blue sky suggestions, it comes down easy
against leaves, sinking
in between blades of grass
as I enter to close
wide-open windows
only to find myself leaning
forward, out, into this home.

from *The End of the Alphabet*

*

In this bed, a man on his back, his eyes graying blue.
It is hurricane season. Sparrows flying in, out the wind.
His lips receiving. He is a shore. The Atlantic rushing.
Clouds opening in the late June storm. This,
as before, in the embrace that takes all my heart.
Imagine his unshaven face, his untrimmed nails, as all

The hurt this world could give.

*

Gnaw. Zigzag. The end of the alphabet buckling floors.
How to come up?

The blue-crown motmot cannot negotiate narrow branches,
but then her wings give way, betray struggle,

intention broken off in puffy cumulus.
I wished him inside again.

Touched him. Feathery
was the refusal,

drawing together what thirsts. His whole self holding me in,
we slept on the edge of overrunning

─────────────────────────────

with parakeets nesting
in porch lights and dying hibiscus covering the ground.

(a dry season choked in dust, etched cracks in dirt roads,
children down from the hills in the sweat of night

to steal water.
                            Plastic containers in those hands,
over the gate to my house. I lie here, my head
on the prime minister's belly, listening: urgency
swallowed by worried stillness

enveloped again by movement, before, finally,
the outside tap turns tentatively on –

*

Ignore your own devastation and it doggedly shadows,
    resurfacing
across the first version, the flat world, forcing you within
the real conversation you hold with yourself.

If abandoned rage asks, *Who should answer for this?*
Say, the very blood of our lives eats composure up.
Or milk on the tongue tasted rude, unfortunate. And hunger

awoke as human. On all sides, riddled. Broken
and broke against. Inside, by earlier years, shook.

I am remembering the hours lived in, steep steps
angled, and the going up and down burdened before
the certain hand went out, pushed –

if only –
or to go again, doing nothing
to stop hurt releasing a body out. We live through, survive

without regard for the self. Forgiving
each day insisting it be forgiven, thinking

our lives umbilical, tied up with living with how far
we can enter into hell and still sit down for Sunday dinner.

*

(then the blond arm, taken
aback, encircles my waist, the long, ready-to-wear
appendage, soothing over

the appeal:

The day I am at peace I will have achieved
a kind of peace even I know suggests I am crazy.
But, as it will be how I survive, I will not feel so.

*

When she arrived

she felt composed. Someone called her. The voice broke,
trying to bridge or to remember. The voice that called
was no other than her own.

*

Did they take a vein from her thigh to mend her heart?
She pulled a pant leg up. Her face, undressed, was more
   interesting.
She was grinning. *How old do you think I am?*

Still she wanted to die. And there, her reflection
facing her. It motioned as if she were alive.
Her photo was in her purse.

*

Da da daa. She repeated,
Da da daa. She wanted to leave.

I got a lot of life for a dead woman.
She laughed. She was laughing. She was lying. The rain.

*

Later in a bar with a friend. He muses: There we were,
two children really.

Later in a bar with only one question. It begins: If we had had
the child – It ends: could he have shielded her from herself?

Later in a bar, he has had a few, he begins: mad, madder than
He ends: Miss. Miss. Understand.

His friend answers only because he thinks he must
but a touch would do – It's a shame. He says: *A shame. A
    shame.*

No one is sad to have saved himself.
He lives. And what is better than a cold beer?

Even with her wet eyelash picking up dust she must realize.

*

Or did she (not he) simply stretch out? She
in reality at peace, face down. Laughing still.
Her body twittering like a machine.

Hard to keep flesh in the mind's eye
when the story
is a mountain range quaking.

from *Plot*

Once Liv thought pregnancy would purify.

* * *

THE EXTENDED ROOT

What comes through the bloodstream to be flushed reduces him to human even as he does not breathe, even as his lids lower to this thick beginning, one-third of an inch below the upper surface of her swirling pit. The place he fills fills with viscid fuel and yet, somehow, does not drown him in the basement membrane of her own convoluted, veined, capillary network, her own ocean of wear. Nourished, coaxed forward in the presence of her whole presence, consequence of her consequences, he is blister of cell, grain named embryo, a climbing substance perceived, absorbing such intimacy as she can offer.

Ersatz   of freehand sketchiness   of hollow form

anonymous   delineation of bone

of moody hue dipped in fetal city   oh so neatly laid

within Liv   estranged interlacing   that she is

Are such seasoned movements truly without desire? Is her organized breath simply indirection as his face forms in his eggplant-purple landscape, the likeness of no other? There now is the peculiar sound of blood flowing, a soft, pulpy *whoosh*, aquatic, the spreading heart-shaped mouth opening into its initialed script. Darkly stained, untidy eyebrows, a mole, blemish-shaped. In the mind's eye never abandoned are the supposed markings on the boy. What is seen before his profile splinters is a face that looks and is certainly startled.

                    How not to smile out loud?

Erland

how not to? when in utero a fetus heartbeat bounces off.
scanned vibrations of this newer soul making a self whole.

how not to? as the chilled gel brings to the screen inked in.
black and white. glimpsed. scrutinized. joy.

Erland

considers this ersatz image. abracadabra and like. so like.
so liked.

by him whose blush tinges with alleluias. so close to life. his
dried lips licked repeatedly.

He's breathing within. but breathless in the red of the ribbon-
cutting. a sunrise.

tickling giddy goodness extracting arrival. here. here is a slip
of fate from a touch that felt right all over.

Erland

in the volumetric space that is him and spilling to become sun-
drenched. impossibly tender.

turning to Liv, love, stands in her way in tinted glasses wanting
slowly to be

received by her who feels survival. its pencil movements.

even as she moves through the still traffic debating.

assuaging doubt.

What do you mean, are we sure?
Just because we are pregnant doesn't mean we have to have it.
What would we be waiting for?
I don't know . . . to be sure?
Liv, are you saying you don't want to have this child?
No . . . no, I am not saying anything. I mean I am just saying
   we could still think about this a little. We still have time.
Time for what? That is what I am not understanding . . .
Time to understand how completely, completely changed our
   lives will be.
Well . . . sure it's scary and things will change, but we will
   have our lives plus the baby. Others have done it. How are
   we so different?
Look, if I can't talk to you about this, who am I to talk to?
I'm sorry I'm happy. I think it will be great. I don't know what
   else to say.

* * *

MILK AND TEARS

Long after she grows tired in the night she hears only the child's
cries. His cries, already recalling, and silence,
the dumbness she wedges herself into.   Cowardly,
and additionally compromised, she hears each cry, punctuating
every space of exception, running through her, meaning to break,
to interrupt each moment attempted. She hears and calls it
silence. Then it is as if the hood of motherhood was meant to
blur herself from herself, a dark cloth dropping over her eyes
until the self of selfless near arose.

NO SOLACE FROM THE TV

*She said she thought it was a dead animal, some wild animal,
'You know, a small animal, killed and buried or . . . or something.'
She didn't know. Just not . . .*

*She said, 'Who would believe that!' She was a woman, she
understood women. This she didn't understand. 'As a woman, as
a mother . . . no, this was not . . . not a mother.'*

*'You could see, anyone could see she was pregnant. We aren't
fools. She can't fool anyone. She was pregnant. Where is the
baby?'*

*'It's hard to know,' he said, 'hard to know now the
psychological state of the mother. We could be looking at
anything from reckless endangerment to . . . to murder. Intent to
murder. But who knows, you know . . . who knows.'*

'Someone . . . someone could be thinking a . . . female with a problem just looking to get rid of the problem. You know, scared of the equation.'

'One could see that this life . . . in this life she might have felt driven to it . . . without choice. A mother, but not a mother really. A woman, but not a mother. A desperate woman or perhaps a woman only.'

In the drift from screen to sleep Liv finds no peace. A woman but not a woman really, in her nightmare she chews at her breasts. Hers is the same sucking sound baby goats make. She examines her flesh-toned spit and molds it into sunglasses. After wearing the glasses for some time, her vision, she notes, is angled downward, cradled by a shadow barely a foot long.

THE DREAM PLAY

Simultaneously and as a consequence, Erland comes to Liv in her dream. His face is flushed. Has he been running?

Where's the baby? he asks.
I haven't got it, she says.
What's in your stomach then?
The blood's run out.
The blood's run out? Where out?
Out, out, and it's taken the thing with it.
Are you mad?
Don't talk about it.
Where's the baby? he shouts.

* * *

PROXIMITY OF STUCK TO TUCK

Liv's own mother had the smell beneath her nails. It convinced her that is how she lost him. He would cover his lips with her hand: the nail seeping the scent of infant. a dry hollowing of appetite. The forgotten kiss –

resigned. dismissed. Finally and once Liv's mother asked,

Why have you let go of my hand?   Her father answered,

I was supposed to go and now I am late.

* * *

Still in play (Act II)

On the street where children now reside, the speed limit is 25.
Green owns the season and will be God. A rain, that was, put
a chill in every leaf, every blade of grass. The red brick, the
asphalt, cold, cold. The front step, the doorknob, the banister,
the knife, the fork. A faucet opens and the woman, Liv, arrives
as debris formed in the sea's intestine, floating in to be washed
ashore and perfumed. In time she opens her mouth and out
rushes, 'Why is the feeling this? Am I offal? Has an unfortunate
accident arrived me here? Does anyone whisper *Stay awhile*, or
the blasphemous *Resemble me, resemble me*?' Those watching
say with their silence, That is Liv, she has styes on her eyes,
or she needs to forget the why of some moment. She doesn't
look right. She is pulling the red plastic handle toward her,
checking around her. She's washing, then watching hands, feet
and shouting *Assemble me. Assemble me.* She is wearing shoes
and avoiding electrical wires, others, steep drops, forgotten
luggage. Those are her dangers. She cannot regret. A hook out of
its eye, she's the underside of a turtle shell. Riveted, and riven,
the others stare, contemplating the proximity of prison to person
before realizing the quickest route *away from* is to wave her on.
They are waving her on. Liv is waved on. Everything remains
but the shouting. A cake is cooling on a rack. Someone is
squeezing out excess water. Another is seasoning with salt. The
blacker cat is in heat. A man sucks the mint in his mouth. The
minutes are letting go. A hose is invisible on the darkened lawn.

In mortal theater (Act IV)

        blessedly the absolute miscarries

and in its release this birth pulls me toward that which is without comparison. in the still water. of green pasture. Lord and Lamb and Shepherd in all circumstances. daylight in increase. always the floating clouds. ceaseless the bustling leaves. we exist as if conceived by our whole lives – the upsurge. its insides. in all our yesterdays. moreover

asking and borne into residence. the life that fills fills in a world without synonym. I labor. this is the applause. This – mercy grown within complexity. and in truth these lies cannot be separated out: I see as deep as the deep flows. I am as willing as is recognized.

        I am.

        am almost to be touching

      * * *

IN PLAY

I am beginning to lose myself, Liv persists.

Fix your face, a tree suggests.

The lines on my face are of the waves originally,
Liv explains.

I see you no matter who, says a cloud.

Still to speak of loss is like dusting a thought much
farther away . . . farther than the moment the atmosphere
cries, I am lost though I am here.

* * *

OR PASSING THE TIME WITH SOME RHYME

Too much within – close the garage, reset
the alarm, let the eye in the world coo.
The River Ouse flows on no matter what
or who gets caught as its debris. She sits
in Le Café for once not distracted
by boo, its bark. She sits rudely sunglassed,
blue silk cascading off her tumultuous
tummy. Honey, are you happy? You there,
indiscriminate, in your loosened dress
skirting sidewalks. You there, flirting across
each shop window though a pastel broach moos
powdered jade, asking, Are you happily –
oh bovine, oh babe – are you happily
charmed? For this world, oh this whorl is a woo.

Just then the woman at the next table said her pregnancy made her feel less lonely and Liv sat up, leaned forward. She removed her sunglasses. The two in conversation looked over and the taller one shifted unconsciously away from Liv's direction. But already Liv was forgotten. The shorter, pregnant woman said again how her pregnancy was a way to put the self she did not like behind her. *Everyone loves me now*, she whispered, and grinned. She lived for this new self the world loved. Expectant, sacred, she felt special. People smiled at her all the time all times of the day. The pregnancy was like an enormous campaign, 'Hello, World!' She liked the world better now that the world loved her. The pregnant woman and her many words expressed this thing. Liv leaned back in her chair. Their conversation had taken a disappointing curve. Not concerned with how much the world loved. Not concerned. The world did not love. Or the world is love. Either way, and yet . . . there had been a beginning . . . *The pregnancy has made me feel less lonely.*

The start had startled her. She held her thought like a photograph before her. A beautiful photograph? A true photograph? Real? Was it a real photograph? The 'true real'. She recalled the phrase from college, the phrase but not its meaning. And wanting a soft sweet, wild strawberries perhaps, Liv left a twenty-dollar bill on the table and walked by the other pregnant woman and her friend out onto the sunlit. She caught her reflection in a shop window – a pregnant woman approaching. *Less lonely?* She considered. Erland, she said aloud, we will be three in a sea of billions. *Less lonely.* First Liv. Then, sometimes, wife. Sometimes mother. Sometimes wife and mother. And still Liv. Liv in guilt. Liv in feeling. Liv creating herself. Liv alone.

Are you awake?

I could be.

I was thinking . . .

Yes?

I was thinking about something I saw today.

Do I have to guess?

A pregnant woman.

You are the pregnant woman.

Umm . . . but I saw another. I saw her from the side, in profile. Her
    stomach really seemed other . . . not essentially her at all . . . not
    something eventually able to substitute for anything, just
    someone else approaching.

And this was a liberating moment?

In that heimlich way that allows the step out of this self into
    myself. Does that make sense?

You mean you saw the child for the first time as other than
    yourself and knew the feeling as true?

Exactly . . . not as a corruptible extension but as that person over
    there. *Apart from* though *a part of.*

Congratulations.

You're sweet.

That same night Erland pressed his ear to Liv's belly.

What do you hear? Liv asked.

Not you, Erland answered. Not you.

from *Don't Let Me Be Lonely: An American Lyric*

There was a time I could say no one I knew well had died. This is not to suggest no one died. When I was eight my mother became pregnant. She went to the hospital to give birth and returned without the baby. Where's the baby? we asked. Did she shrug? She was the kind of woman who liked to shrug; deep within her was an everlasting shrug. That didn't seem like a death. The years went by and people only died on television – if they weren't Black, they were wearing black or were terminally ill. Then I returned home from school one day and saw my father sitting on the steps of our home. He had a look that was unfamiliar; it was flooded, so leaking. I climbed the steps as far away from him as I could get. He was breaking or broken. Or, to be more precise, he looked to me like someone understanding his aloneness. Loneliness. His mother was dead. I'd never met her. It meant a trip back home for him. When he returned he spoke neither about the airplane nor the funeral.

/

Every movie I saw while in the third grade compelled me to ask, Is he dead? Is she dead? Because the characters often live against all odds it is the actors whose mortality concerned me. If it were an old, black-and-white film, whoever was around would answer yes. Months later the actor would show up on some late-night talk show to promote his latest efforts. I would turn and say – one always turns to say – You said he was dead. And the misinformed would claim, I never said he was dead. Yes, you did. No, I didn't. Inevitably we get older; whoever is still with us says, Stop asking me that.

Or one begins asking oneself that same question differently. Am I dead? Though this question at no time explicitly translates into Should I be dead, eventually the suicide hotline is called. You are, as usual, watching television, the eight-o'clock movie, when a number flashes on the screen: 1–800–SUICIDE. You dial the number. Do you feel like killing yourself? the man on the other end of the receiver asks. You tell him, I feel like I am already dead. When he makes no response you add, I am in death's position. He finally says, Don't believe what you are thinking and feeling. Then he asks, Where do you live?

Fifteen minutes later the doorbell rings. You explain to the ambulance attendant that you had a momentary lapse of happily. The noun, happiness, is a static state of some Platonic ideal you know better than to pursue. Your modifying process had happily or unhappily experienced a momentary pause. This kind of thing happens, perhaps is still happening. He shrugs and in turn explains that you need to come quietly or he will have to restrain you. If he is forced to restrain you, he will have to report that he is forced to restrain you. It is this simple: Resistance will only make matters more difficult. Any resistance will only make matters worse. By law, I will have to restrain you. His tone suggests that you should try to understand the difficulty in which he finds himself. This is further disorienting. I am fine! Can't you see that! You climb into the ambulance unassisted.

On the bus two women argue about whether Rudy Giuliani had to kneel before the Queen of England when he was knighted. One says she is sure he had to. They all had to, Sean Connery, John Gielgud, Mick Jagger. They all had to. The other one says that if he had, they would have seen it on television. We would have seen him do it. I am telling you we would have seen it happen.

When my stop arrives I am still considering Giuliani as nobility. It is difficult to separate him out from the extremes connected to the city over the years of his mayorship. Still, a day after the attack on the World Trade Center a reporter asked him to estimate the number of dead. His reply – More than we can bear – caused me to turn and look at him as if for the first time. It is true that we carry the idea of us along with us. And then there are three thousand dead and it is incomprehensible and ungraspable. Physically and emotionally we cannot bear it, should in fact never have this capacity. So when the number is released it is a sieve that cannot hold the loss Giuliani recognized and answered for.

Wallace Stevens wrote, 'the peculiarity of the imagination is nobility ... nobility which is our spiritual height and depth; and while I know how difficult it is to express it, nevertheless I am bound to give a sense of it. Nothing could be more evasive and inaccessible. Nothing distorts itself and seeks disguise more quickly. There is a shame of disclosing it and in its definite presentation a horror of it. But there it is.'

Sir Rudolph kneeling. It was apparently not something to be seen on television, but rather a moment to be heard and experienced; a moment that allowed his imagination's encounter with death to kneel under the weight of the real.

/

Walking home I find myself singing softly, to the tune of 'Day-O', *Come Mister Taliban give us bin Laden.* This version of the song along with its accompanying animation was passed on to me via e-mail and now I can't stop myself.

I am walking behind two big guys. One says to the other,

> I don't regret any part of my life. It's been a good life. Were anything to happen I could live with that.

I think he means he could live with his own death. I want to tell him he won't have to.

At the airport-security checkpoint on my way to visit my grandmother, I am asked to drink from my water bottle.

This water bottle?

That's right. Open it and drink from it.

/

At the airport-security checkpoint on my way to visit my grandmother, I am asked to take off my shoes.

Take off my shoes?

Yes. Both please.

/

At the airport-security checkpoint on my way to visit my grandmother, I am asked if I have fever.

A fever? Really?

Yes. Really.

/

My grandmother is in a nursing home. It's not bad. It doesn't smell like pee. It doesn't smell like anything. When I go to see her, as I walk through the hall past the common room and the nurses' station, old person after old person puts out his or her hand to me. Steven, one says. Ann, another calls. It's like being in a third-world country, but instead of food or money you are what is wanted, your company. In third-world countries I have felt overwhelmingly American, calcium-rich, privileged, and white. Here, I feel young, lucky, and sad. Sad is one of those words that has given up its life for our country, it's been a martyr for the American dream, it's been neutralized, co-opted by our culture to suggest a tinge of discomfort that lasts the time it takes for this and then for that to happen, the time it takes to change a channel. But sadness is real because once it meant something real. It meant dignified, grave; it meant trustworthy; it meant exceptionally bad, deplorable, shameful; it meant massive, weighty, forming a compact body; it meant falling heavily; and it meant of a color: dark. It meant dark in color, to darken. It meant me. I felt sad.

from *Citizen: An American Lyric*

I

When you are alone and too tired even to turn on any of your devices, you let yourself linger in a past stacked among your pillows. Usually you are nestled under blankets and the house is empty. Sometimes the moon is missing and beyond the windows the low, gray ceiling seems approachable. Its dark light dims in degrees depending on the density of clouds and you fall back into that which gets reconstructed as metaphor.

The route is often associative. You smell good. You are twelve attending Sts Philip and James School on White Plains Road and the girl sitting in the seat behind asks you to lean to the right during exams so she can copy what you have written. Sister Evelyn is in the habit of taping the 100s and the failing grades to the coat closet doors. The girl is Catholic with waist-length brown hair. You can't remember her name: Mary? Catherine?

You never really speak except for the time she makes her request and later when she tells you you smell good and have features more like a white person. You assume she thinks she is thanking you for letting her cheat and feels better cheating from an almost white person.

Sister Evelyn never figures out your arrangement perhaps because you never turn around to copy Mary Catherine's answers. Sister Evelyn must think these two girls think a lot alike or she cares less about cheating and more about humiliation or she never actually saw you sitting there.

/

The rain this morning pours from the gutters and everywhere else it is lost in the trees. You need your glasses to single out what you know is there because doubt is inexorable; you put on your glasses. The trees, their bark, their leaves, even the dead ones, are more vibrant wet. Yes, and it's raining. Each moment is like this – before it can be known, categorized as similar to another thing and dismissed, it has to be experienced, it has to be seen. What did he just say? Did she really just say that? Did I hear what I think I heard? Did that just come out of my mouth, his mouth, your mouth? The moment stinks. Still you want to stop looking at the trees. You want to walk out and stand among them. And as light as the rain seems, it still rains down on you.

/

A friend argues that Americans battle between the 'historical self' and the 'self self'. By this she means you mostly interact as friends with mutual interest and, for the most part, compatible personalities; however, sometimes your historical selves, her white self and your black self, or your white self and her black self, arrive with the full force of your American positioning. Then you are standing face-to-face in seconds that wipe the affable smiles right from your mouths. What did you say? Instantaneously your attachment seems fragile, tenuous, sub-ject to any transgression of your historical self. And though your joined personal histories are supposed to save you from misunderstandings, they usually cause you to understand all too well what is meant.

/

The new therapist specializes in trauma counseling. You have only ever spoken on the phone. Her house has a side gate that leads to a back entrance she uses for patients. You walk down a path bordered on both sides with deer grass and rosemary to the gate, which turns out to be locked.

At the front door the bell is a small round disc that you press firmly. When the door finally opens, the woman standing there yells, at the top of her lungs, Get away from my house! What are you doing in my yard?

It's as if a wounded Doberman pinscher or a German shepherd has gained the power of speech. And though you back up a few steps, you manage to tell her you have an appointment. You have an appointment? she spits back. Then she pauses. Everything pauses. Oh, she says, followed by, oh, yes, that's right. I am sorry.

I am so sorry, so, so sorry.

III

Not long ago you are in a room where someone asks the philosopher Judith Butler what makes language hurtful. You can feel everyone lean in. Our very being exposes us to the address of another, she answers. We suffer from the condition of being addressable. Our emotional openness, she adds, is carried by our addressability. Language navigates this.

For so long you thought the ambition of racist language was to denigrate and erase you as a person. After considering Butler's remarks, you begin to understand yourself as rendered hypervisible in the face of such language acts. Language that feels hurtful is intended to exploit all the ways that you are present. Your alertness, your openness, and your desire to engage actually demand your presence, your looking up, your talking back, and, as insane as it is, saying please.

/

Another friend tells you you have to learn not to absorb the world. She says sometimes she can hear her own voice saying silently to whomever – you are saying this thing and I am not going to accept it. Your friend refuses to carry what doesn't belong to her.

You take in things you don't want all the time. The second you hear or see some ordinary moment, all its intended targets, all the meanings behind the retreating seconds, as far as you are able to see, come into focus. Hold up, did you just hear, did you just say, did you just see, did you just do that? Then the voice in your head silently tells you to take your foot off your throat because just getting along shouldn't be an ambition.

V

Sometimes 'I' is supposed to hold what is not there until it is. Then *what is* comes apart the closer you are to it.

This makes the first person a symbol for something.

The pronoun barely holding the person together.

Someone claimed we should use our skin as wallpaper knowing we couldn't win.

You said 'I' has so much power; it's insane.

And you would look past me, all gloved up, in a big coat, with fancy fur around the collar, and record a self saying, you should be scared, the first person can't pull you together.

Shit, you are reading minds, but did you try?

Tried rhyme, tried truth, tried epistolary untruth, tried and tried.

You really did. Everyone understood you to be suffering and still everyone thought you thought you were the sun – never mind our unlikeness, you too have heard the noise in your voice.

Anyway, sit down. Sit here alongside.

/

Leaving the day to itself, you close the door behind you and pour a bowl of cereal, then another, and would a third if you didn't interrupt yourself with the statement – you aren't hungry.

Appetite won't attach you to anything no matter how depleted you feel.

It's true.

You lean against the sink, a glass of red wine in your hand and then another, thinking in the morning you will go to the gym having slept and slept beyond the residuals of all yesterdays.

Yes, and you do go to the gym and run in place, an entire hour running, just you and

your body running off each undesired desired encounter.

STOP-AND-FRISK

Script for Situation video created in collaboration with John Lucas

I knew whatever was in front of me was happening and then the police vehicle came to a screeching halt in front of me like they were setting up a blockade. Everywhere were flashes, a siren sounding and a stretched-out roar. Get on the ground. Get on the ground now. Then I just knew.

And you are not the guy and still you fit the description because there is only one guy who is always the guy fitting the description.

/

I left my client's house knowing I would be pulled over. I knew. I just knew. I opened my briefcase on the passenger seat, just so they could see. Yes officer rolled around on my tongue, which grew out of a bell that could never ring because its emergency was a tolling I was meant to swallow.

In a landscape drawn from an ocean bed, you can't drive yourself sane – so angry you are crying. You can't drive yourself sane. This motion wears a guy out. Our motion is wearing you out and still you are not that guy.

/

Then flashes, a siren, a stretched-out roar – and you are not the guy and still you fit the description because there is only one guy who is always the guy fitting the description.

Get on the ground. Get on the ground now. I must have been speeding. No, you weren't speeding. I wasn't speeding? You didn't do anything wrong. Then why are you pulling me over? Why am I pulled over? Put your hands where they can be seen. Put your hands in the air. Put your hands up.

Then you are stretched out on the hood. Then cuffed. Get on the ground now.

/

Each time it begins in the same way, it doesn't begin the same way, each time it begins it's the same. Flashes, a siren, the stretched-out roar –

Maybe because home was a hood the officer could not afford, not that a reason was needed, I was pulled out of my vehicle a block from my door, handcuffed and pushed into the police vehicle's backseat, the officer's knee pressing into my collar-bone, the officer's warm breath vacating a face creased into the smile of its own private joke.

Each time it begins in the same way, it doesn't begin the same way, each time it begins it's the same.

Go ahead hit me motherfucker fled my lips and the officer did not need to hit me, the officer did not need anything from me except the look on my face on the drive across town. You can't drive yourself sane. You are not insane. Our motion is wearing you out. You are not the guy.

/

This is what it looks like. You know this is wrong. This is not what it looks like. You need to be quiet. This is wrong. You need to close your mouth now. This is what it looks like. Why are you talking if you haven't done anything wrong?

And you are not the guy and still you fit the description because there is only one guy who is always the guy fitting the description.

/

In a landscape drawn from an ocean bed, you can't drive yourself sane – so angry you can't drive yourself sane. The charge the officer decided on was exhibition of speed. I was told, after the fingerprinting, to stand naked. I stood naked. It was only then I was instructed to dress, to leave, to walk all those miles back home. And still you are not the guy and still you fit the description because there is only one guy who is always the guy fitting the description.

Script for Public Fiction at Hammer Museum

On the train the woman standing makes you understand there are no seats available. And, in fact, there is one. Is the woman getting off at the next stop? No, she would rather stand all the way to Union Station.

The space next to the man is the pause in a conversation you are suddenly rushing to fill. You step quickly over the woman's fear, a fear she shares. You let her have it.

The man doesn't acknowledge you as you sit down because the man knows more about the unoccupied seat than you do. For him, you imagine, it is more like breath than wonder; he has had to think about it so much you wouldn't call it thought.

When another passenger leaves his seat and the standing woman sits, you glance over at the man. He is gazing out the window into what looks like darkness.

You sit next to the man on the train, bus, in the plane, waiting room, anywhere he could be forsaken. You put your body there in proximity to, adjacent to, alongside, within.

You don't speak unless you are spoken to and your body speaks to the space you fill and you keep trying to fill it except the space belongs to the body of the man next to you, not to you.

Where he goes the space follows him. If the man left his seat before Union Station you would simply be a person in a seat on the train. You would cease to struggle against the unoccupied seat when where why the space won't lose its meaning.

You imagine if the man spoke to you he would say, it's okay, I'm okay, you don't need to sit here. You don't need to sit and you sit and look past him into the darkness the train is moving through. A tunnel.

All the while the darkness allows you to look at him. Does he feel you looking at him? You suspect so. What does suspicion mean? What does suspicion do?

The soft gray-green of your cotton coat touches the sleeve of him. You are shoulder to shoulder though standing you could feel shadowed. You sit to repair whom who? You erase that thought. And it might be too late for that.

It might forever be too late or too early. The train moves too fast for your eyes to adjust to anything beyond the man, the window, the tiled tunnel, its slick darkness. Occasionally, a white light flickers by like a displaced sound.

From across the aisle tracks room harbor world a woman asks a man in the rows ahead if he would mind switching seats. She wishes to sit with her daughter or son. You hear but you don't hear. You can't see.

It's then the man next to you turns to you. And as if from inside your own head you agree that if anyone asks you to move, you'll tell them we are traveling as a family.

VI

When the waitress hands your friend the card she took from you, you laugh and ask what else her privilege gets her? Oh, my perfect life, she answers. Then you both are laughing so hard, everyone in the restaurant smiles.

/

'The subject of so many films is the protection of the victim, and I think, I don't give a damn about those things. It's not the job of films to nurse people. With what's happening in the chemistry of love, I don't want to be a nurse or a doctor, I just want to be an observer.'

As a child, Claire Denis wished to be a nurse; she is no longer a child. Years have passed and so soon we love this world, so soon we are willing to coexist with dust in our eyes.

Denise Riley

from *Marxism for Infants*

There's nothing for it   Your 'father' and I
Biologically, a lack   The child tries manfully
He calls it special seed but he gets confused at school

An unselfconscious wife is raised high as a flag over
                the playground and burns up

In 1970

The eyes of the girls are awash with violets
pansies are flowering under their tongues
they are grouped by the edge of the waves and are anxious

to swim;

each one is on fire with passion to achieve herself.

Not What You Think

wonderful light
viridian summers
deft boys
no thanks

Lure, 1963

Navy near-black cut in with lemon, fruity bright lime green.
I roam around around around around acidic yellows, globe
oranges burning, slashed cream, huge scarlet flowing
anemones, barbaric pink singing, radiant weeping When
will I be loved? Flood, drag to papery long brushes
of deep violet, that's where it is, indigo, oh no, it's in
his kiss. Lime brilliance. Obsessive song. Ink tongues.
Black cascades trail and spatter darkly orange pools
toward washed lakes, whose welling rose and milk
beribboned pillars melt and sag, I'm just a crimson
kid that you won't date. Pear glow boys. Clean red.
Fluent grey green, pine, broad stinging blue rough
strips to make this floating space a burning place of
whitest shores, a wave out on the ocean could never
move that way, flower, swell, don't ever make her blue.
Oh yes I'm the great pretender. Red lays a stripe of darkest
green on dark. My need is such I pretend too much, I'm
wearing. And you're not listening to a word I say.

A Misremembered Lyric

A misremembered lyric: a soft catch of its song
whirrs in my throat. 'Something's gotta hold of my heart
tearing my' soul and my conscience apart, long after
presence is clean gone and leaves unfurnished no
shadow. Rain lyrics. Yes, then the rain lyrics fall.
I don't want absence to be this beautiful.
It shouldn't be; in fact I know it wasn't, while
'everything that consoles is false' is off the point –
you get no consolation anyway until your memory's
dead; or something never had gotten hold of
your heart in the first place, and that's the fear thought.
Do shrimps make good mothers? Yes they do.
There is no beauty out of loss; can't do it –
and once the falling rain starts on the upturned
leaves, and I listen to the rhythm of unhappy pleasure
what I hear is bossy death telling me which way to
go, what I see is a pool with an eye in it. Still let
me know. Looking for a brand-new start. Oh and never
notice yourself ever. As in life you don't.

Shantung

It's true that anyone can fall
in love with anyone at all.
Later, they can't. Ouf, ouf.

How much mascara washes away each day
and internationally, making the blue one black.
Come on everybody. Especially you girls.

Each day I think of something about dying.
Does everybody? do they think that, I mean.
My friends! some answers. Gently
unstrap my wristwatch. Lay it face down.

Well All Right

Above, a flurry of swans, brothers, great wings airy
around my bowed head in rushing darkness, neatly
these bone fingers plaited their green cloaks each night
to unfeather them so now they stand upright before me
freed and gaily they leap to their caparisoned horses as
in my breathing cell I smooth down my own cloak of
nettles – but Grimm sweetie mediaeval Griseldas, right
out on the night plains are no tiny lights of huddlement
but only the impersonal stars in blackness and the long
long winds. What you see is what you see: it's never
what you don't. Well all right, things happened it would
be pleasanter not to recall, as a deeply embarrassed dog
looks studiedly at a sofa for just anything to do instead,
so determine to assume events silently with no fuss –
who doesn't try to – yes that is a dart in my neck and
doesn't it look a bit biedermeier – so take up that thud
of attack dropped out of a righteously wide-open beak
sailing slowly across its own high sky which you'd not
registered as contempt straight out to kill – far rather
than know that, wear it as an owned cloak's blazing
fabric stuck in the fine flesh of your shoulders like any
natural skin burning; so cloaked, no one sees through
to you wrapped in darkness, only a darkness pressed to
outward navy twill – no queen of the night's gorgeous
winking suit, just suave cheap unexceptional off any
rack – want to slip out of it? but flesh has soaked to join
its fiery choric costume. Break out in flames. Leap to
the crests of orange birds flickering along the long line
of shoulders, hiss, warble in gaping whistles hoarse lyre
chants of plumed and swollen throats whose glowing trills
waver and zigzag the swayed neck heavy under the flare
song of any body glittering with hard memory. Let fall

this garment with its noisy wings. Slide from me now –
and let's just run something red and stinging rapidly down
the page, shall we, let's try an echt gloss speed placing
let's stand back in triumph dripping brushes, shall we
see what can be made out of this lot my lot, its lovely
trailed gash wet as a frock in a pool, what it's for is for
defence, it will keep your beautiful soul glazed as a
skein of floating hill mist and as quietly as slightly
and as palely lit – at risk of frank indifference it may
make beauty to sleep and, or, to sleep with. Who sang
'you don't have to die before you live' – well who.

Poem Beginning with a Line from Proverbs

As iron sharpens iron
I sharpen the face of my friend
so hard he sings out
in high delicate notes.

A struggle for mastery to most speak
powerful beauty would run any
attention or kindness clean out
of town in angry rags.

Ringed by darkness the heart pulsates.
And power comes in like lightning.
A lion in the room, fair and flowing
twists with unsparing eyes.

Whitely the glance runs
to it and away. But let it
talk its golden talk if we
don't understand it.

Grabbed by remote music
I'm frightening myself. Speak
steadily as is needed to
stare down beauty. That calms it.

Lyric

Stammering it fights to get
held and to never get held
as whatever motors it swells
to hammer itself out on me

then it can call out high
and rounded as a night
bird's cry falling clean
down out of a black tree.

I take on its rage at the cost
of sleep. If I love it I sink
attracting its hatred. If I
don't love it I steal its music.

Take up a pleat in this awful
process and then fold me flat
inside it so that I don't see
where I was already knotted in.

It is my burden and subject
to listen for sweetness in hope
to hold it in weeping ears though
each hurt each never so much.

So Is It?

Opening mouth up to sifting rain, blurred to an o,
crouched to the green wash, swooping water,
stone arches slit to wind-cropped turf, in a grip
turn as sea-slicing gannets cut shock fans of
white water. Held shudder, sluiced in low cloud.
Where is a steady place where work gets fairly done.
Straight speech can drop out from behind the teeth
or the hands shake out clean strokes from bunched
knots onto energetic white or long soft ropes of
line loop from the mouth, uncoil to columns
hollowed to poured sheen purity, only in shelter.
Some. I walk into a light hot wood. Inside it all
exhales, a sulky wind gets up, slings a sad mass
at the back of eyes lowered for chattering dusk,
fingers dried ochres in rough air brushed rustling
to cream hoops, strokes powdery blues tacked on
to black wire. Die deeper into life at every second.
And no self coating slips onto my papers to make
them pulse to rooms emptied of me, they'll bear no
faint film for my children to wipe off later, so solidly
do objects stay themselves – the handwriting of the
freshly dead doesn't get any loopier or more
archaic, as waxed comb honey would seep through
knuckles or pine ooze stiffen, domed to wasps.
Things packed with what they are. Not slatted I.
Preserve a self, for what? for ice through the ribs,
pale splinters driven straight to the heart's meat.
Calf of my senses. I'd thought out ways to grasp –
have walked straight off their edges. To dreams
of silent towns, nights, doorways, gazes, radios
on, while here a man turns and turns towards his

windows, staring out over the street at dusk as rain-hemmed curtains sway, their blackening yellowed net. All seek a piercing charm to throb gingerly nursed in our hands like a bird. Dear heart don't be so strange to me but be nature. Or give me a sudden bluish look. If I can get this far. An oil spill on the wet road swims outwards, pleats, and flashes lilac or rusting orange at its rim where it will dry and darken. I think that's it. As I must think it is like this for you – it is, isn't it. Don't tell me that edge that I never believe.

Song

Some very dark blue hyacinths on the table
A confession or two before dusk
flings open the fridge with loud relief
Listen honey I . . .

A warm disturbing wind cruises the high road

where in curtained rooms children
are being beaten then so am I again but no one's
asking for it, I'm asking for something different now

Rayon

The day is nervous buff – the shakiness, it is inside the day or me?
Perhaps the passions that we feel don't quite belong to anyone
but hang outside us in the light like hoverflies, aping wasps
                                                    and swivelling
and lashing up one storm of stripes. In tiny cones of air.
Yet you enact that feeling, as you usually *bzzzzzzzzz* get to do
                                                    it, while I,
I do this. If it takes me all night and day. Oh Carol.

Dark Looks

Who anyone is or I am is nothing to the work. The writer
properly should be the last person that the reader or the listener need think about
yet the poet with her signature stands up trembling, grateful, mortally embarrassed
and especially embarrassing to herself, patting her hair and twittering If, if only
I need not have a physical appearance! To be sheer air, and mousseline!
and as she frets the minute wars scorch on through paranoias of the unreviewed
herded against a cold that drives us in together – then pat me more, Coventry
to fall from Anglo-Catholic clouds of drifting *we*'s high tones of feeling down
to microscopic horror scans of tiny shiny surfaces rammed up against the nose
cascading on Niagara, bobbed and jostled, racing rusted cans of Joseph Cotten reels
charmed with his decent gleam: once *we* as incense-shrouded ectoplasm gets blown
fresh drenched and scattered units pull on gloss coats to preen in their own polymer:
still it's not right to flare and quiver at some fictive 'worldly boredom of the young'
through middle-aged hormonal pride of *Madame, one must bleed; it's necessary . . .*
Mop mop georgette. The only point of holding up my blood is if you'd think So what?
We've all got some of that: since then you'd each feel better; less apart. – Hardly:
it's more for me to know that *I* have got some, like a textbook sexual anxiety

while the social-worker poet in me would like her revenge for having been born and left.
What forces the lyric person to put itself on trial though it must stay rigorously uninteresting?
Does it count on its dullness to seem human and strongly lovable; a veil for the monomania
which likes to feel itself helpless and touching at times? Or else it backs off to get sassy
since arch isn't far from desperate: So take me or leave me. No, wait, I didn't mean leave
me, wait, just *don't* – or don't flick and skim to the foot of a page and then get up to go –

from Seven Strangely Exciting Lies

III OLEANNA

I'd thought you'd get through any disagreement just by talking
by persisting quietly. Fool. Steel-rimmed the hole at the centre
through which all hopes of contact plummet down in flames
as modes of talk criss-cross from opposite directions like jets
                                                    in flight
which rightly never slow or swerve to read the fleecy trails of
                                                    others
then something searing wipes its arc across my sight again
as rape fields of acrylic flowers do stripe your eyeballs yellow
and unreflecting green takes charge at the horizon threatening
                                                    to rain –
shove off or I soak you sunshine – suppose you stopped
                                                    describing
something, would stopping free you from it, almost as if it
                                        hadn't happened?
So is that shiver down the back of the neck water, or is it
                                        memory calling water
or is it squaring up to getting properly shredded, which does
                                        cut clean away
from iron edges soaking into rust, from blurring fiery wells
                                        of tin-work –
someone calling tell them I'm not home, hurt me so bad to see
                                        my baby get
away, ashen-mouthed, smoking regret – instead of all that
                                        tactile surface junk
there is this sobbing flash, you-die immediacy: who longs for
                                        decent
and consensual talk, it is that calm and democratic front I'd
                                        work to be:
I was not born to that.

VII DISINTEGRATE ME

There was such brilliance lifting off the sea, its aquamarine strip
blocked in behind white-dashed mimosas, that it stung my eyes
all morning as I stood in the old playground, pushing the swing
steadily, looking out across the water and longing to do without
these radio voices, and without my post as zealous secretary, as
transmitter of messages from the dead, who'd issue disclaimers
that they'd ever sent them – all the while a slow hot cut spreads
to baste me now with questions of my own complicity in harm
muttering thoughtfully about 'patterns' until I'm stamped out as
an old paisley shawl or worn kelim, do I look good as this one
or should I be less loud, or less repetitive? and on the top of my
wardrobe, familiar spirits cluster and hang to chatter, lean over
to peer down interestedly at me, vivaciously complaining about
the large amounts of fluff I've left up there, 'that's just as we'd
expect': meanwhile the out-to-kill person is not, or so she or he
shrugs, pulled at by voices, but dead at heart stands amnesiac
plumped out with the effective innocence of the untroubled –
This gloss is taking me on unconvincing dashes down blind
alleys I mistrust, since desperate to see things straight, I can't fit
apt blame in to self-damnation: could I believe instead in drained
abandon, in mild drift out over some creamy acre studded with
brick reds, to be lifted, eased above great sienna fields and born
onward to be an opened stem or standing hollow, a flesh ring
through which all slips or a fluent cylinder washed through by
azure-tangled braid, trailing Stella Maris, fervent star of the sea
marine milk vessel flopped at the lip flicking down swathes of
gulls emulsifying blackened earth striped and coiled under rock
under burnt straw air fuzzed in breathy fields of coconut-sharp
gorse flowers flushed tan on cliffs where lower, toothpaste green
lucidly rears and rears in the crash of blinding crumpled water

smoothing to clear and flat; so calmly let me disperse so simply
let me disperse, drawn out thin-frothed in a broad lacy pancake
fan of salt, or let me fall back as dolphins rock back in the sea
twirled like slow toys on pin-wheels – No single word of this
is any more than decoration of an old self-magnifying wish
to throw the self away so violently and widely that interrogation
has to pause since its chief suspect's sloped off to be cloud, to be
wavery colour bands: no 'release from service to a hard master'
said of the thankful close, it's hoped, of sexual need in oldest age
can touch this other drive of shame fighting to clear a name
                                                            to itself:
it can't, because its motor runs on a conviction that if I
                                                    understood
my own extent of blame then that would prove me agent; it
                                                        doesn't
want to face a likely truth of helplessness – that the inflated
                                                        will to
gauge and skewer each wrong turn may blank out what's
                                                    far worse
to bear: impersonal hazard, the humiliating lack of much
                                                    control –
I don't get past this thought with any confidence.

A Part Song

i

You principle of song, what are you *for* now
Perking up under any spasmodic light
To trot out your shadowed warblings?

Mince, slight pillar. And sleek down
Your furriness. Slim as a whippy wire
Shall be your hope, and ultraflexible.

Flap thinly, sheet of beaten tin
That won't affectionately plump up
More cushioned and receptive lays.

But little song, don't so instruct yourself
For none are hanging around to hear you.
They have gone bustling or stumbling well away.

ii

What is the first duty of a mother to a child?
At least to keep the wretched thing alive – Band
Of fierce cicadas, stop this shrilling.

My daughter lightly leaves our house.
The thought rears up: *fix in your mind this*
Maybe final glimpse of her. Yes, lightning could.

I make this note of dread, I register it.
Neither my note nor my critique of it
Will save us one iota. I know it. And.

iii

Maybe a retouched photograph or memory,
This beaming one with his striped snake-belt
And eczema scabs, but either way it's framed,
Glassed in, breathed hard on, and curated.
It's odd how boys live so much in their knees.
Then both of us had nothing. You lacked guile
And were transparent, easy, which felt natural.

iv

Each child gets cannibalized by its years.
It was a man who died, and in him died
The large-eyed boy, then the teen peacock
In the unremarked placid self-devouring
That makes up being alive. But all at once
Those natural overlaps got cut, then shuffled
Tight in a block, their layers patted square.

v

It's late. And it always will be late.
Your small monument's atop its hillock
Set with pennants that slap, slap, over the soil.
Here's a denatured thing, whose one eye rummages
Into the mound, her other eye swivelled straight up:
A short while only, then I come, she carols – but is only
A fat-lot-of-good mother with a pointless alibi: 'I didn't
Know.' Yet might there still be some part for me
To play upon this lovely earth? Say. Or
Say *No*, earth at my inner ear.

vi

A wardrobe gapes, a mourner tries
Her several styles of howling-guise:

You'd rather not, yet you must go
Briskly around on beaming show.

A soft black gown with pearl corsage
Won't assuage your smashed ménage.

It suits you as you are so pale.
Still, do not get that saffron veil.

Your dead don't want you lying flat.
There'll soon be time enough for that.

vii

Oh my dead son you daft bugger
This is one glum mum. Come home I tell you
And end this tasteless melodrama – quit
Playing dead at all, by now it's well beyond
A joke, but your humour never got cruel
Like this. Give over, you indifferent lad,
Take pity on your two bruised sisters. For
Didn't we love you. As we do. But by now
We're bored with our unproductive love,
And infinitely more bored by your staying dead
Which can hardly interest you much, either.

viii

Here I sit poleaxed, stunned by your vanishing
As you practise your charm in the underworld
Airily flirting with Persephone. Not so *hard*
To imagine what her mother *had gone through*
To be ferreting around those dark sweet halls.

ix

They'd sworn to stay for ever but they went
Or else I went – then concentrated hard
On the puzzle of what it ever truly *meant*
For someone to be here then, just like that,
To not. Training in mild loss was useless
Given the final thing. And me lamentably
Slow to 'take it in' – far better toss it out,
How should I take in such a bad idea. No,
I'll stick it out instead for presence. If my
Exquisite hope can wrench you right back
Here, resigned boy, do let it as I'm waiting.

x

I can't get sold on reincarnating you
As those bloody 'gentle showers of rain'
Or in 'fields of ripening grain' – oooh
Anodyne – nor yet on shadowing you
In the hope of eventually pinpointing
You bemused among the *flocking souls*
Clustered like bats, as all thronged gibbering
Dusk-veiled – nor in modern creepiness.
Lighthearted presence, be bodied forth
Straightforwardly. Lounge again under
The sturdy sun you'd loved to bake in.
Even ten seconds' worth of a sighting
Of you would help me get through
This better. With a camera running.

xi

Ardent bee, still you go blundering
With downy saddlebags stuffed tight
All over the fuchsia's drop earrings.
I'll cry 'Oh bee!' to you, instead –
Since my own dead, apostrophized,
Keep mute as this clear garnet glaze
You're bumping into. Blind diligence,
Bee, or idiocy – this banging on and on
Against such shiny crimson unresponse.

xii

Outgoing soul, I try to catch
You calling over the distances
Though your voice is echoey,

Maybe tuned out by the noise
Rolling through me – or is it
You orchestrating that now,

Who'd laugh at the thought
Of me being sung in by you
And being kindly dictated to.

It's not like hearing you live was.
It is what you're saying in me
Of what is left, gaily affirming.

xiii

Flat on a cliff I inch toward its edge
Then scrutinize the chopped-up sea
Where gannets' ivory helmet skulls
Crash down in tiny plumes of white
To vivify the languid afternoon –
Pressed round my fingertips are spikes
And papery calyx frills of fading thrift
That men call sea pinks – so I can take
A studied joy in natural separateness.
And I shan't fabricate some nodding:
'She's off again somewhere, a good sign.
By now, she must have got over it.'

xiv

Dun blur of this evening's lurch to
Eventual navy night. Yet another
Night, day, night, over and over.
I so want to join you.

xv

The flaws in suicide are clear
Apart from causing bother
To those alive who hold us dear
We could miss one another
We might be trapped eternally
Oblivious to each other
One crying *Where are you, my child*
The other calling *Mother*.

xvi

Dead, keep me company
That sears like titanium
Compacted in the pale
Blaze of living on alone.

xvii

Suspended in unsparing light
The sloping gull arrests its curl
The glassy sea is hardened waves
Its waters lean through shining air
Yet never crash but hold their arc
Hung rigidly in glaucous ropes
Muscled and gleaming. All that
Should flow is sealed, is poised
In implacable stillness. Joined in
Non-time and halted in free fall.

xviii

It's all a resurrection song.
Would it ever be got right
The dead could rush home
Keen to press their chinos.

xix

She do the bereaved in different voices
For the point of this address is to prod
And shepherd you back within range
Of my strained ears; extort your reply
By finding any device to hack through
The thickening shades to you, you now
Strangely unresponsive son, who were
Such reliably kind and easy company,
Won't you be summoned up once more
By my prancing and writhing in a dozen
Mawkish modes of reedy piping to you
– Still no? Then let me rest, my dear.

XX

My sisters and my mother,
Weep dark tears for me
I drift as lightest ashes
Under a southern sea

O let me be, my mother
In no unquiet grave
My bone-dust is faint coral
Under the fretful wave

Tree seen from bed

The fuller leaves are ridged, the newer red.
Sunshine is pooled over them, like lacquer.
One branch catches a notion of movement,
shivering, then the rest cotton on in a rush
roused by the wind, to thrash and vacillate.
A toss-up, where they'll all go next – to lash
around through summer until autumn, that
is where; to fall. May it be managed lightly
though it could well turn wilder beforehand.
Tree watched from my sickbed, read to me.
Read from the hymnal of frank life – of how
to be old, yet never rehearse that fact cosily.

Clemency

Sweet goose, fat on spring's
fine ideals, hiss in a lime sauce –

clemency's glow is rueful, citrine-
veined, then always ends up being

about practical kindness – don't tut!
That's brilliantly green and airy

& will frogmarch some right round
under the blinking sun so look lively.

Under the Answering Sky

I can manage being alone,
can pace out convivial hope
across my managing ground.
Someone might call, later.

What do the dead make of us
that we'd flay ourselves trying
to hear them though they may
sigh at such close loneliness.

I would catch, not my echo,
but their guarantee that this
bright flat blue is a mouth
of the world speaking back.

There is no depth to that blue.
It won't 'bring the principle
of darkness with it', but hums
in repose, as radiant static.

Silent Did Depart

'A spirit casts no shadow' – true, of the filmy dead.
Not of a living creature tapering itself to an obelisk.
Rocky mute, life's too serious for this not speaking!
Don't be stuccoed so hard over any humane seepage.

What had been churning round in that ardent pillar?
You'd not have dreamed an upright man could petrify.
Drape my anointing hair at the feet of superb cement.
All hindsight shakes itself out vigorously like a wet dog.

Listening for Lost People

Still looking for lost people – look unrelentingly.
'They died' is not an utterance in the syntax of life
where they belonged, no *belong* – reanimate them
not minding if the still living turn away, casually.
Winds ruck up its skin so the sea tilts from red-blue
to blue-red: into the puckering water go his ashes
who was steadier than these elements. Thickness
of some surviving thing that sits there, bland. Its
owner's gone nor does the idiot howl – while I'm
unquiet as a talkative ear. Spring heat, a cherry
tree's fresh bronze leaves fan out and gleam – to
converse with shades, yourself become a shadow.
The souls of the dead are the spirit of language:
you hear them alight inside that spoken thought.

And Another Thing

Some new arrival's coming, whose name may not be happy.
Attend it. Childishly lovely, once, to listen to anyone new
as if even the oldest harm was outgrown as a liberty bodice.
Does sifting through damage ease, or enshrine it; how grasp
a past, but not skid on embittered accounting? The ledgers
exhibit their black surplus malice and red lack of tenderness,
while 'suffering' easily gets competitive as each suspects hers
was the rougher lot, yet feels shy out of shame at her history
that won't dovetail with her present. Hoist personalized flags
though they're so stiff with encrusted blood they'd first need
a good sousing in tears? – forget that. Could the years have
been easier if you'd just settled early on hating a sex instead,
although which one of them to begin with? Sleeked up your
plumes to swan out and ruffle your usual vexers of dailiness?
Filed reports to the muses, via cicadas' surveillance, on men
who weren't rapt, only dozing in warm grass at noon, lulled
by music to dreaming their sonic enchantment is virtuously
militant, a sparkly art stance plus a strong civic end in itself?
It's late. 'You must live as you can', which is all we ever did.

Boxy Piece

Exhibit of small boxes made from wood
to house their thought and each an open
coffin of the not-dead with their chirring.
Satin-lined frames stack square in blocks
nested to a columbarium – then mumble,
closet doves, whose fond carpenter drills
piercings for more air, won't let you flap.

'All, as a rule, fall towards their wound'

Sheathed in their amber, dove grey, olive silk
saints clutch a grill or wheel, pincers or spear.
Calm heads anointed by the buttery sunlight
incline to these instruments of their torture
turned to starred, yet unvarnished, blazons
as cloaks drip carmine and rose velvets glow.
Here the raised axe is no more than its action:
it hands the decapitated to their merciful rest.
Would it help me a bit to stroke its mild blade,
take the edge off old violence – though not gild
it later, announcing that 'blessedly, I survived' –
what hope is there of a purely secular grace?
Attend, Agnes; your white emblem's bleating.

Never to Disinter the Pink Companion

Never to disinter the pink companion. Wintry. So isn't everyone
drawn to human warmth, if only by animal curiosity? Seems not.
Then how pleasantly to give back his enigma of wordless absence
to its real owner, like a jacket he'd not realized he'd left behind?
Worse, he had: 'Thanks a lot for another trip to the charity shop.'
To confess my bafflement with grace. So, tolerant Grace, though
I've needed to call for you so often, please don't ignore my knocks
but uncoil from your couch and ease out of your door, smiling, to
me mulish with a little scar literature, it is a very late form of love.

Death Makes Dead Metaphor Revive

Death makes dead metaphor revive,
Turn stiffly bright and strong.
Time that is felt as 'stopped' will freeze
Its to-fro, fro-to song

I parrot under feldspar rock
Sunk into chambered ice.
Language, the spirit of the dead,
May mouth each utterance twice.

Spirit as echo clowns around
In punning repartee
Since each word overhears itself
Laid bare, clairaudiently.

An orphic engine revs but floods
Choked on its ardent weight.
Disjointed anthems dip and bob
Down time's defrosted spate.

Over its pools of greeny melt
The rearing ice will tilt.
To make *rhyme* chime again with *time*
I sound a curious lilt.

Maggie Nelson

After a Fight

Fuck you too, my less compassionate self
says quietly. You've never really

respected me anyway, especially not now
that I refuse to be the keeper

of your anger, the messy pall
of it, from where we kill

what we can't suck. Still
I have faith in the healthy ink

of ideograms, the little cone of flame
nudged about by the wind.

My pillow book would list
such beautiful things, your heart

would die to read them.

The Poem I Was Working On Before
September 11, 2001

after Louise Bourgeois

Say something awful, say
'She leaned on the fork'

Say something beautiful, say
'Eyes smudged with soft kohl'

Now lead the way under
the spiders, yes under the spiders

where a bad woman rules. Glassy
white eggs in a wrought-iron

grid – she almost goes through
with it. Engulfed in a perfect

day, the pressure lifts –
urban life is OK as long as

there is still wind, something new
to breathe, though do you want

to know what that strange smell is
Well I'll tell you it's the fumigation

of the lizards in the subway system,
KEEP CLEAR, DO NOT INHALE

O you're so gullible. But can I breathe here – where? –
in this tiny circle, where the homunculus

is hopping on the gamelan and playing
the song of joyful death – just think

about that. Say something nice, say
'Your sexiness is necessarily an aporia,

but that just means nothing can ever
demolish it.' Now that we're grown up

and have no willpower (of all things!)
The absurdity is I hope this will never, ever end –

not the banging on the can, not the dark brown liquid
in the blue glass. I love it here, on earth – I don't care a fig

for what comes next, which is exactly what
the suicide bomber said of the Israelis he killed yesterday

at the discotheque. There is something bestial
in me, it wants to be drunk on saliva, and

there is something ugly about me, which has to do
with my fear of dying of hives. But above all

there is something very lovely about today,
the day I wandered beneath a great spider

and the city opened itself up as if to apologize
for its heat and changing ways.

Don't sit there slobbering all over
the thermometer! The least you could do

is try to capture an enigma with an image,
or don't sweat it – out West my mother

is fondling the stone bellies of the Three Graces.
She waters everything at night now, she is

the night-gardener, she goes out with a flashlight
and looks for insects doing their deeds. Looks

for all that oozes underneath. Yesterday I saw
a man burn a strip of skin off his arm –

he just threw the skin in the trash
and for a moment we all stood there, staring

at the bright white streak on his arm. It didn't look like
anything. Then the red blood started to perk up

around the edges, it was quite eerie and beautiful,
it was the skin under the skin, it was

the flesh. Our flesh is often so red
in the photos that get taken of us, and I admit

that something about life overheats me, but nothing like
the teenager who overdosed on Ecstasy and was found

on her kitchen floor with a body temperature of 104 degrees.
I saw it on the News, the News whose job it is to scare me.

It would seem by such a lead story that
these are decadent and peaceful times, but there is

much else. But the rest doesn't count. The bottom half
always drops out, as George W. dines along the Venice canal.

But today – just today – I felt new for the first time this century –
no one noticed me – I was unsexed! – I stood

in front of *Les Demoiselles d'Avignon*;
I could take it or leave it. I read Dr Williams

in the park, he says the sun parts the clouds
like labia (I guess he would know). Looking up

from my book I became momentarily afraid
of the polar situations that may arise between us,

but then I let it all go. I'm tired of small dry things.
I want to nestle into the clammy crack

between conscience and id – speaking of which,
I'm so glad you turned me on to donut peaches –

they will taste like this summer until
they taste like next summer, but why

think about that yet? You never let me see you naked
but when you do it is like a rain of almonds, your soft spots

smell so tart and floral, and you don't pull me into you often
but when you do you pull me into you. All of this

is worth fighting for. We may be called upon
to do so, in which case there will be no more Ovaltine,

no therapy, no crackers. Praying is just thinking
about nothing, or trying not to think about

the lines of cows, their fat nipples squeezed
into the machines. (I'm surprised the milk

still comes out!) Through a hole in my head I imagine
my brain seeping out, in shell-pink ribbons

as the village moderates itself into night:
bottles are getting recycled, objects are left behind

in moving vehicles, people remove their earrings and
    war-paint
and get ready to sleep. Tomorrow is Saturday,

and the city will rise. There could be a planet out there
whose inhabitants are watching our demise, but enough

already about the living dead! There may be
neither space nor time in the space and time

in which I love you, and thus our love
will remain iridescent forever, and have only

as much sternness as the universe has to offer
(which may or may not be much). There *is* a world

that I think, but it is not different from this one.
The great spider and her shadow, the clouds

moving across the mirrored Cineplex – they're real, too.

Train to Coney Island

This time I'm going all the way to the Mermaid Parade, I only wish
I were a photographer! It's late, I hope the floats won't be dismantled.
Last night I dreamt that L. and I got married but our audience
was not behaving – Jennifer Miller the bearded lady kept yapping. In real life
I splintered up and asked M. for a second chance: 'I'll change,' etc.
We are all equally deceived, perhaps, by ourselves. One thing I know for sure:
it's pointless to hope I have an encylopedic mind. All it ever retains
is the bare-bones sentiment of the thing, the hiss of information
rushing off into the canyon. I don't really mind, words chip off the block
and float in summer air. They're nothing compared to the buttery rings
of Saturn! & I have always been a sucker for mystification. Here we are
at Neptune Avenue! It's funny and a little sad that I've written such a chatty,
prosy sonnet, as all I wanted was to take the train to its final destination
and write a teeny chiseled poem, some perfect illumination

the future of poetry

the poetry of the future has got to have a lot of nerve. it's got to come from at least three brains: the brain in the head, the gut-brain, and the brain in the ovaries. it will wax red and rise bone-white. the poetry of the future will be nutritious and opulent. justifications for its existence will no longer be interesting: lenin loved beethoven. the poetry of the future will glitter like a scimitar. the poetry of the future will be unabashedly adolescent. it will get younger as it gets older. it will reflect the interests of both carnivores and herbivores. it will be as heterogeneous as it is misguided. the poetry of the future will watch blue branches shaking in winter and red canyons gaping in the sun. it will send a space shuttle full of representative poems to a gaseous planet where upon exiting the shuttle the poems will turn into gorgeous multicolored rocks that can live without water. the poetry of the future will wear squeaky shoes in the vatican. it will say where we work and who we love and what we eat. sometimes it will be hungover and desperate. it might bite its nails. tired of being on the lam, it might have to choose between giving itself up to the authorities or going out in a blaze of glory. the poetry of the future will be so enormous that it will only be visible from an aerial perspective. many will believe it to be a message from aliens. the poetry of the future will be so expensive and in demand that it will disrupt the global economy as we know it. as no one will ever be fully awake to the miracle of our existence its work will never be done. sometimes the poetry of the future will have to put on a silk kimono and sigh. sometimes it will need to fuck like a bunny. other times it will have to walk 29 miles to visit a grave. it will have bones to excavate and houses to rebuild. the poetry of the future might worry it will die from weeping. it might have to send a root down to come up. sometimes it will put on a head-lamp and go looking for urchins. at times the poetry of the future will be nothing more than red eyes caught in a flash photograph or the memory of percussion. the poetry of the future will compete with advertising and lose. it will then be run by a secret society of cave-fish that have never needed to develop eyes. it will retreat to a hearth made of mud and eat beans with its family in a comfortable silence. the poetry of the future will be the last sad sack to leave the party. the poetry of the future will be written by women. it will accept chance as its engine. it will have a front row seat at the cinema. it will be vigorously imperfect. the poetry of the future will live in a redwood tree for 2 years if it feels it has to make a point. it will understand that seeds must stay scattered. the poetry of the future will say, last stop, everybody off! once we get off the poetry of the future will set us on a scavenger hunt in which the first thing we have to find is our own idea of utopia. the poetry of the future will come home sopping wet after thinking things through and ask for a second chance. the poetry of the future might take a vow of silence. the poetry of the future will know everything there is to know as soon as it is born. above all, the poetry of the future will do whatever the hell it wants.

my life as an exchange student

for puri y las gemelas

teenage girls in the style of 'heavy'
dance with their faces an inch from the wall

I am a virgin in the way
that hurts, and life feels consistently

intense: the tan face of danny
at la cuadra, he seems so worldly

the streaked hair of the town slut
who is on 'la pastilla'

I am not on la pastilla but all the same
they will eventually call me una desgracia

(how would he know, my spanish father
who worked all day at renault)

those were the days of pepper trees, when
I was unsure if anyone would ever love me

and afraid I would die of acne
in a foreign country. each dusk I waded

in the ankle-high cotton that floated in
from portugal across the fetid river

where we weren't allowed to swim
(it had something to do with franco).

I didn't die there, though I could have
or later swirling underwater in the dirty

mediterranean, all fucked up on sherry
after giving first fellatio by a hotel pool

(not our hotel, we'd hopped the fence)
we woke up on lawn chairs in the mist

I don't really know if any of this actually happened
or who those guys with the self-inflicted tattoos were, anyway

ever since then I'm a little afraid of madrid
I was jealous of all the girls, their beauty

the brunette from L.A. and my botticelli angel, amy
I thought a lot about free will and siouxsie

who would have thought
my future friends would be

so percussive, that I would live so long
in one american city, or that I would learn to like

the dick stuffed in my face.

The Earth in April

You wanted me to be

      overwhelmed by magnolia

and so I was, fat white buds

      perched

like flocks frozen

      a moment before flight

It's spring, you whispered

      She's going to be alright

from *Jane: A Murder*

[Jane's journal]

Dear

I understand many people write for therapy – one's own.
So this epistle, addressed to no one,
is therapy for me. What have I got to say –
oh a lot of crazy impressions about nothing
I imagine

FROM THE LIGHT OF THE MIND (FOUR DREAMS)

She had been shot once in the front and once in the back of the head. She wandered, trying to find someone to remove the slugs from her skull. She was not dead yet, but she feared she was dying. The holes in her head were perfectly round and bloodless, with blunt-flared edges, two eclipses. The passage of air through the holes felt peculiar, just dimly painful, like chewing hot or cold food on a cavity, the sensation of space where it had once been dense and full.

Sunlight shot around the circumference of each black rind, so that a long shaft of pale light cast out from the center of her forehead, and another shaft streamed behind her.

Is this the light of the mind? Is this the light of __my__ mind?

So I was a genius after all! The thought made her smile, but then she wondered, *Why had the light always been invisible? I must have been squandering it, I must have felt only its vaguest rotations. Now what can I do with it? If I could find a lamp-shade, someone could read by it. I might illuminate entire rooms, entire dungeons, I shine so bright.*

But in fact she was losing the light; it leaked everywhere, unstoppable.

* * *

TWO WRONGS

They say elephants can recognize the bones of a dead loved one when they stumble upon them in the wild. They will stop and wander around the huge decaying bones, swinging their trunks, braying in despair.

The voice-over on TV might say, *The elephants know that these are the bones of Dolly. They are mourning the loss of Dolly.* But Dolly is our name, not theirs.

It feels different to mourn something without naming its name. A fetus, a snake you call Snake, a woman with no Social Security number and the commonest of names.

She was born in Muskegon, Michigan, on February 23, 1946, and she died on March 20, 1969, sometime between midnight and two a.m.

I was born four years later, almost to the day.

Her grave has no epitaph, only a name.

I found her in the wild; her name was Jane, plain Jane.

* * *

REFRAIN

'Agreeing that [Jane] was a "liberal," [a friend] said, "She was interested in seeing that the black students got the things they wanted."'
— Ann Arbor News, *March 22, 1969*

My relatives all say
Jane wanted to change the world

Then they add
None of us can

* * *

THE LAW

By her senior year, Jane was on the pill.
She knew that if her parents found out

they would not think her worthy
of their money, so she cut herself off –

applied to law school without telling anyone.
She got in, won a fellowship, and went.

Despite her misgivings about the profession
(*Lawyers are a breed – detestable at times,* she wrote)

she threw herself into her work. The *Ann Arbor News*
later wrote, 'Students at the law school described [Jane]

as a serious, studious person who liked to talk about school
but not about her personal life.' Both Jane and Phil

shielded each other from their parents; neither family
would have accepted the union of Gentile and Jew.

She must have been madly in love with you, I say
to Phil. *Oh,* he smiles, *I don't know about that.*

Well, I say, *madly enough to consider
spending the rest of her life with you.*

Oh that, he laughs. *That's just plain mad.*

* * *

FROM PHIL'S PHOTOS
3. SILVER LAKE

And here she is
at Silver Lake, in

a two-piece swim-
suit, navy blue

with white stripes
up the side. She's sitting

on a pink blanket, along
with several books

and a pair of wet
moccasins. Phil's body

makes a shadow in
the lower left corner;

it's clear that to take the picture
he must be standing

in the water. The space
he vacated on the blanket

is wet with blobs of
body-shaped wetness,

the beach so narrow
that the water is flooding

them, flooding Jane's feet
and calves, flooding

the pink blanket.
The whole photo

is dreamy, as if washed
in milk, Jane's skin

a pale apricot and
glowing. And I love it,

this lush, fuzzy sliver
in which two people

once spread out
on damp sand

and loved one another.

* * *

ORDER OF EVENTS

The autopsy report confirmed
that all strangulation occurred

after she was already dead
from two shots in the head.

I don't know how they know.

Part of me thinks they tell you so
so you don't split off –

charred flakes starting to drift
in a bone-black madness

* * *

DEMOGRAPHICS

'All the victims have been independent and politically liberal,'
the paper said, i.e. girls who would be God.

Three 'coeds', a graduate student in art, an eighth-grader, a
    runaway, a law student.

The world is ours, but we walk in it
noticed.

* * *

(1960)

   [Jane's diary]

If only life and death were better understood by me.
I dread and fear death and yet am uncertain of life and the
    why of it.
I have yet to have real faith, believe and follow without
    question.

When I can accept time, life, and death,
I will be ready for the responsibilities of adulthood
and will step into them easily and with confidence.

Now I am but a wondering, confused individual.

A Halo over the Hospital

You looked beautiful
Your eyes blue and lucid
Though your face has been reconstructed
by a team of surgeons, just a few little scars
on the bridge of your nose
and under your chin, you'd never know
your skin hung on a rack
and they gave you titanium cheekbones
and a titanium jaw, I couldn't tell either
until I brushed your teeth
trying hard to dislodge the morning's oatmeal
while avoiding the broken ones
Some in the front are apparently little stumps
and inside your gums, an astonishing gnarl of metal
Such miniature machinery! You are truly
a cyborg now, the metal of your jaw linking up
with the metal of your cheekbones, behind the scenes
Now your skull is literally shining. And your arms
can move much more than I thought, and your grace
is utterly intact. But your mouth gets so dry,
I have to trace your delicate lips
with a finger laden with balm, cherry balm
from a tube, make sure my hands are clean
then reapply, reapply. And give you water
from a miniature green sponge on a stick,
a little lollipop of water. *This is*
an incredibly inefficient means of drinking
you observe, and indeed each suck gives you
only a thimbleful. So we have to perform
the feat thousands of times
Try going in through the left side, you advise
and I straddle your bed to do so, trying

to avoid your broken tooth in the front
Just shove it right back in there, you tell me, always
the mentor, always encouraging me
to get it right, to use an adequate angle
and thrust. When you sleep I make sure
you stay breathing, make sure I'm there
when you open your eyes, as you're slightly stricken
upon remembering the prison
your body has become. *I'm frightened*, you say
Then *I'm sad, so sad to be paralyzed,* and I'm sad too
You can't wipe away your tears because your hands
don't move, and I can't wipe them away either
because it's too abrupt a motion, everything now
needs to happen very slowly. So we place
a wet towel across your eyes and the tears
must soak upwards. More ice, more ice, the water
on the little green sponge has to be cold, not
lukewarm, and your fingertips can't touch
the sheet, it's too painful to touch something smooth
OK we'll try propping your hands up
on rough white towels, is that better, yes
You say my hand feels good touching yours
and it's like I won the lottery. You fall asleep again
and I hold your hand, but don't know where
to put my head, so I lay it on your bed beside your hips
and fall asleep too. It's Sunday afternoon. Outside
in the common room there are people
we once might have pitied but now we envy –
double-knee replacement, one amputated arm, big deal
Later I get to wheel you outside, it takes forever
to lift you into the chair and requires a motorized
yellow crane, your body like a beautiful tan bird
in its beak. I try to wheel you slowly like Nurse Peggy said
Slowly down the glass hallways, careful not to raise

your blood pressure, we can go out into the autumn air
but we can't go down to the pond, not yet, you say
you want to see the trees with the gold leaves and so
we do, the leaves fallen along the pathway bunch up
in the wheels of the chair and I get a little panicked,
how do you work this thing, where are the brakes?
Everyone at home wants to know if you are OK
You're not 'OK', you're paralyzed and in tremendous pain
Everyone keeps asking, *Do you think she will walk again?*
But that really isn't the issue, the issue today
is your distended stomach, your painful little balloon of gas
Apparently the spine runs the bowels and the blood
and just about everything else, miraculous and hurt
jelly cord. Your whole body suddenly withered
    and transparent
We can see your muscles move with the electrodes on
You have some tricep, no bicep, your left quad jerked
but no luck on the right, someday you'll recover, I just know it
and I tell you so, I can't stop smoothing your hair, its
blonde laced with gray, growing longer
than it's ever been, and your body
I always wanted to see naked, now
I've seen it twice: once in a photo album
I stumbled upon, photos of you and your lover
naked in your kitchen, you both looked
happy and free, and I felt happy for you
and now here, the aureole of your immobile breast
magnanimous and wide, your legs quiet
and hairy, so not-moving. We discover
some stitches in your calf, someone at the ICU
must have forgotten about them, the nurse pushes on them
and pus comes out, we all wince. They have to come out soon
and so they do. Dinner wheels in, puréed tuna melt, puréed
Black Forest cake, and I imagine this gigantic medieval kitchen

where they make each dish then send it
to an enormous blender and out comes
this ridiculous beige & gray paste. Of course
you're not hungry, the lemon yoghurt I fed you
so assiduously in the morning has caused you
unthinkable pain, and to think I pushed you into
eating all of it, agony. I read you an essay of mine
about troubling the passage from the particular to the universal
and you say yes, Maggie, the problem now is to think
the singular. The singular, you say again, very seriously
as if it's ten years prior and we're just sitting in your office
This whole situation is seeming very singular, there's a book
you want me to read but you can't remember the title
so we have to call J., I hold the phone up to your ear
Press it harder, you say, OK, it's called PROVINCIALIZING
    EUROPE
and I promise to read it, at this point
I'd eat a copy of MEIN KAMPF if you asked me to
I am so sad to be paralyzed
The problem now is to think the singular
The pain is returning and thank God Nurse Winnie
is back on duty, I'm so glad she's curious and presses you
to be articulate, even when you're tired and don't feel like it
She needs more of a description, she doesn't want
you to get an infection, finally you say *Winnie, the pain*
in my intestine is coming from my unconscious, a line
that brings me unending happiness. Later I sit on the bed
and tell you a little about my spastic love life, about the person
I am trying not to be in love with
You ask if we went home and fucked, I say we did
and you are happy, and I love the way the word *Fuck*
comes out of your wired mouth, as if desire can never be
closed down or tortured out, as if *Fuck* will always bubble out
of a metal forest. I tell you a little more

and you say, *Good for fucking, bad for future planning*
You say I don't have to be ashamed of my desire
Not for sex, not for language
You say you've learned by age fifty
that you need them both, together, and that you and J.
have that. You've been so happy. Crying now you say
All I can think is that if we built it once
we can build it again and I know you will and tell you so, then kiss
your forehead, the one part of your body
that hasn't sustained any damage
Not one single scratch on your helmet
You took the whole fucking fall
on your chin, the snap back of your head
caused the fracture, the space that's injured
is no bigger than a chocolate bar and yet
here we are. Jelly cord swollen with broken blood
vessels, thousands of nerve cells fighting for life
'Scars form, further distorting any surviving nerve pathways'
'One axon after another turns into a severed stump'
Fuck science, it's so moralistic, and the terrible sensations mean
you will heal because you can feel, like when the nurse
pushed on your stitches until they oozed and you said *Ow*
or when the smoothness of the sheet assails your fingertips
or when you say everything, absolutely everything
feels so tired and sore. Every word a chore, and yet
you give me so many, we discuss direct service
vs. community organizing, your care for the world
simply astonishing. You even make your physical therapist
feel beautiful, by expounding on the virtues
of her new haircut. *Well my husband really likes it,* she says
and you don't even cringe. You change the subject, tell us
the story of your first dog, whose name was
Shameless Hussy. I am happy to see so many competent people
buzzing around your body, I get angry when they move you

too quickly, I like it when they tend to you
tenderly, your head kind of tacked on by a brace
I hate this thing, you say, *but I'm so terrified*
to have it come off, because you know you can't hold
your own head up, it's like being an infant again
but you have all this rich language. And when
they take it off to stretch your head
your neck finally appears, beautiful and clammy
and bluish, a little like the plucked skin of a bird
You ask me to lift your shoulders off the pillow
then set them back down, I try to get the rolled towel
behind your head with one hand while I redistribute
the gelatin of the pillow with the other, *Be a little bolder,* you say
What feels right to you keeps changing
Thousands of times I moisten your mouth with balm
and water. At lights out I drive back to your house
where I sleep on the floor of your office, amidst
the hundreds of projects you left in-progress
Piles of books and papers, tracts about
global feminism, calls for social justice
I cry a little then, in mourning for
your graceful and butch handwriting
But I know now where you are, and where you will be
for some time, gold leaves swirling outside
your window, gold leaves making a halo
A halo over the hospital

from *Bluets*

1. Suppose I were to begin by saying that I had fallen in love with a color. Suppose I were to speak this as though it were a confession; suppose I shredded my napkin as we spoke. *It began slowly. An appreciation, an affinity. Then, one day, it became more serious. Then* (looking into an empty teacup, its bottom stained with thin brown excrement coiled into the shape of a sea horse) *it became somehow <u>personal</u>.*

2. And so I fell in love with a color – in this case, the color blue – as if falling under a spell, a spell I fought to stay under and get out from under, in turns.

* * *

14. I have enjoyed telling people that I am writing a book about blue without actually doing it. Mostly what happens in such cases is that people give you stories or leads or gifts, and then you can play with these things instead of with words. Over the past decade I have been given blue inks, paintings, postcards, dyes, bracelets, rocks, precious stones, watercolors, pigments, paperweights, goblets, and candies. I have been introduced to a man who had one of his front teeth replaced with lapis lazuli, solely because he loved the stone, and to another who worships blue so devoutly that he refuses to eat blue food and grows only blue and white flowers in his garden, which surrounds the blue ex-cathedral in which he lives. I have met a man who is the primary grower of organic indigo in the world, and another who sings Joni Mitchell's *Blue* in heartbreaking drag, and another with the face of a derelict whose eyes literally leaked blue, and I called this one the prince of blue, which was, in fact, his name.

15. I think of these people as my blue correspondents, whose job it is to send me reports from the field.

16. But you talk of all this jauntily, when really it is more like you have been mortally ill, and these correspondents send pieces of blue news as if last-ditch hopes for a cure.

* * *

18. A warm afternoon in early spring, New York City. We went to the Chelsea Hotel to fuck. Afterward, from the window of our room, I watched a blue tarp on a roof across the way flap in the wind. You slept, so it was my secret. It was a smear of the quotidian, a bright blue flake amidst all the dank providence. It was the only time I came. It was essentially our lives. It was shaking.

19. Months before this afternoon I had a dream, and in this dream an angel came and said: *You must spend more time thinking about the divine, and less time imagining unbuttoning the prince of blue's pants at the Chelsea Hotel.* But what if the prince of blue's unbuttoned pants *are* the divine, I pleaded. *So be it,* she said, and left me to sob with my face against the blue slate floor.

20. *Fucking leaves everything as it is. Fucking may in no way interfere with the actual use of language. For it cannot give it any foundation either. It leaves everything as it is.*

* * *

22. Some things do change, however. A membrane can simply rip off your life, like a skin of congealed paint torn off the top of a can. I remember that day very clearly: I had received a

phone call. A friend had been in an accident. Perhaps she would not live. She had very little face, and her spine was broken in two places. She had not yet moved; the doctor described her as a 'pebble in water'. I walked around Brooklyn and noticed that the faded periwinkle of the abandoned Mobil gas station on the corner was suddenly blooming. In the baby-shit yellow showers at my gym, where snow sometimes fluttered in through the cracked gated windows, I noticed that the yellow paint was peeling in spots, and a decent, industrial blue was trying to creep in. At the bottom of the swimming pool, I watched the white winter light spangle the cloudy blue and I knew together they made God. When I walked into my friend's hospital room, her eyes were a piercing, pale blue and the only part of her body that could move. I was scared. So was she. The blue was beating.

* * *

50. The confusion about what color is, where it is, or whether it is persists despite thousands of years of prodding at the phenomenon. And literally prodding: in his zeal, in the 'dark chamber' of his room at Trinity College, Newton at times took to sticking iron rods or sticks in his eyes to produce then analyze his perceptions of color. Children whose vision has been damaged have been known to smash their fingers into their eyes to recreate color sensations that have been lost to them. (*That's the spirit!*)

* * *

52. Try, if you can, not to talk as if colors emanated from a single physical phenomenon. Keep in mind the effects of all the various surfaces, volumes, light-sources, films, expanses, degrees of solidity, solubility, temperature, elasticity, on color.

Think of an object's capacity to emit, reflect, absorb, transmit, or scatter light; think of 'the operation of light on a feather'. Ask yourself, what is the color of a puddle? Is your blue sofa still blue when you stumble past it on your way to the kitchen for water in the middle of the night; is it still blue if you don't get up, and no one enters the room to see it? Fifteen days after we are born, we begin to discriminate between colors. For the rest of our lives, barring blunted or blinded sight, we find our-self face-to-face with all these phenomena at once, and we call the whole shimmering mess 'color'. You might even say that it is the business of the eye to make colored forms out of what is essentially shimmering. This is how we 'get around' in the world. Some might also call it the source of our suffering.

53. 'We mainly suppose the experiential quality to be an intrin-sic quality of the physical object' – this is the so-called systematic illusion of color. Perhaps it is also that of love. But I am not willing to go there – not just yet. I believed in you.

* * *

71. I have been trying, for some time now, to find dignity in my loneliness. I have been finding this hard to do.

72. It is easier, of course, to find dignity in one's solitude. Lone-liness is solitude with a problem. Can blue solve the problem, or can it at least keep me company within it? – Not, not exactly. It cannot love me that way; it has no arms. But sometimes I do feel its presence to be a sort of wink – *Here you are again*, it says, *and so am I.*

74. Who, nowadays, watches the light stream through the walls of her 'dark chamber' with the company of a phantasma-goric assistant, or smashes at her eyes to reproduce lost color

sensations, or stays up all night watching colored shadows drift across the walls? At times I have done all of these things, but not in service of science, nor of philosophy, not even of poetry.

75. Mostly I have felt myself becoming a servant of sadness. I am still looking for the beauty in that.

* * *

90. Last night I wept in a way I haven't wept for some time. I wept until I aged myself. I watched it happen in the mirror. I watched the lines arrive around my eyes like engraved sunbursts; it was like watching flowers open in time-lapse on a windowsill. The tears not only aged my face, they also changed its texture, turned the skin of my cheeks into putty. I recognized this as a rite of decadence, but I did not know how to stop it.

91. *Blue-eye*, archaic: 'a blueness or dark circle around the eye, from weeping or other cause.'

92. Eventually I confess to a friend some details about my weeping – its intensity, its frequency. She says (kindly) that she thinks we sometimes weep in front of a mirror not to inflame self-pity, but because we want to feel witnessed in our despair. (*Can a reflection be a witness? Can one pass oneself the sponge wet with vinegar from a reed?*)

93. 'At first glance, it seems strange to think that an innocuous, inborn behavior such as crying could be dysfunctional or symptomatic,' writes one clinical psychologist. But, this psychologist insists, we must face the fact that some crying is simply 'maladaptive, dysfunctional, or immature.'

94. – Well then, it is as you please. This is the dysfunction talking. This is the disease talking. This is how much I miss you talking. This is the deepest blue, talking, talking, always talking to you.

95. But please don't write again to tell me how you have woken up weeping. I already know how you are in love with your weeping.

96. For a prince of blue is a prince of blue because he keeps 'a pet sorrow, a blue-devil familiar, that goes with him everywhere' (Lowell, 1870). This is how a prince of blue becomes a pain devil.

from *The Argonauts*

October, 2007. The Santa Ana winds are shredding the bark off the eucalyptus trees in long white stripes. A friend and I risk the widowmakers by having lunch outside, during which she suggests I tattoo the words HARD TO GET across my knuckles, as a reminder of this pose's possible fruits. Instead the words *I love you* come tumbling out of my mouth in an incantation the first time you fuck me in the ass, my face smashed against the cement floor of your dank and charming bachelor pad. You had *Molloy* by your bedside and a stack of cocks in a shadowy unused shower stall. Does it get any better? *What's your pleasure?* you asked, then stuck around for an answer.

Before we met, I had spent a lifetime devoted to Wittgenstein's idea that the inexpressible is contained – inexpressibly! – in the expressed. This idea gets less air time than his more reverential *Whereof one cannot speak thereof one must be silent,* but it is, I think, the deeper idea. Its paradox is, quite literally, *why I write,* or how I feel able to keep writing.

For it doesn't feed or exalt any angst one may feel about the incapacity to express, in words, that which eludes them. It doesn't punish what can be said for what, by definition, it cannot be. Nor does it ham it up by miming a constricted throat: *Lo, what I would say, were words good enough.* Words are good enough.

It is idle to fault a net for having holes, my encyclopedia notes.

A day or two after my love pronouncement, now feral with vulnerability, I sent you the passage from *Roland Barthes by Roland Barthes* in which Barthes describes how the subject who utters the phrase 'I love you' is like 'the Argonaut renewing his ship during its voyage without changing its name.' Just as the *Argo*'s parts may be replaced over time but the boat is still called the *Argo*, whenever the lover utters the phrase 'I love you,' its meaning must be renewed by each use, as 'the very task of love and of language is to give to one and the same phrase inflections which will be forever new.' I thought the passage was romantic. You read it as a possible retraction. In retrospect, I guess it was both.

* * *

When making your butch-buddy film, *By Hook or By Crook*, you and your cowriter, Silas Howard, decided that the butch characters would call each other 'he' and 'him', but in the outer world of grocery stores and authority figures, people would call them 'she' and 'her'. The point wasn't that if the outer world were schooled appropriately re: the characters' preferred pronouns, everything would be right as rain. Because if the outsiders called the characters 'he', it would be a different kind of he. Words change depending on who speaks them; there is no cure. The answer isn't just to introduce new words (*boi, cisgendered, andro-fag*) and then set out to reify their meanings (though obviously there is power and pragmatism here). One must also become alert to the multitude of possible uses, possible contexts, the wings with which each word can fly. Like when you whisper, *You're just a hole, letting me fill you up.* Like when I say *husband.*

* * *

By February I was driving around the city looking at apartment after apartment, trying to find one big enough for us and your son, whom I hadn't yet met. Eventually we found a house on a hill with gleaming dark wood floors and a view of a mountain and a too-high rent. The day we got the keys, we slept together in a fit of giddiness on a thin blanket spread out over the wood floor of what would become our first bedroom.

That view. It may have been a pile of rough scrub with a stagnant pond at its top, but for two years, it was our mountain.

* * *

During our first forays out as a couple, I blushed a lot, felt dizzy with my luck, unable to contain the nearly exploding fact that I've so obviously gotten everything I'd ever wanted, everything there was to get. *Handsome, brilliant, quick-witted, articulate, forceful, you.* We spent hours and hours on the red couch, giggling, *The happiness police are going to come and arrest us if we go on this way. Arrest us for our luck.*

What if where I am is what I need? Before you, I had Deborah always thought of this mantra as a means of making Hay peace with a bummer or even catastrophic situation. I never imagined it might apply to joy, too.

* * *

I have long known about madmen and kings; I have long known about feeling real. I have long been lucky enough to *feel* real, no matter what diminishments or depressions have come my way. And I have long Sara known that the *moment of queer pride is a refusal to be* Ahmed *shamed by witnessing the other as being ashamed of you.*

* * *

On one of the long afternoons that has since bled into the one long afternoon of Iggy's infancy, I watch him pause on all fours at the threshold to our backyard, as he contemplates which scraggly oak leaf to scrunch toward first with his dogged army crawl. His soft little tongue, always whitened in the center from milk, nudges out of his mouth in gentle anticipation, a turtle bobbing out of its shell. I want to pause here, maybe forever, and hail the brief moment before I have to jump into action, before I must become the one who eliminates the *inappropriate object,* or, if I'm too late, who must harvest it from his mouth.

You, reader, are alive today, reading this, because someone once adequately policed your mouth exploring. In the face of this fact, Winnicott holds the relatively unsentimental position that we don't owe these people (often women, but by no means always) anything. But we do owe *ourselves* 'an intellectual recognition of the fact that at first we were (psychologically) absolutely dependent, and that absolutely means absolutely. Luckily we were met by ordinary devotion.'

By ordinary devotion, Winnicott means ordinary devotion. 'It is a trite remark when I say that by devoted I simply mean devoted.' Winnicott is a writer for whom ordinary words are good enough.

* * *

There's something truly strange about living in a historical moment in which the conservative anxiety and despair about queers bringing down civilization and its institutions (marriage, most notably) is met by the anxiety and despair so many queers feel about the failure or incapacity of queerness to bring down civilization and its institutions, and their frustration with the assimilationist, unthinkingly neoliberal bent of the mainstream GLBTQ+ movement, which has spent fine coin begging entrance into two historically repressive structures: marriage and the military. 'I'm not the kind of faggot who wants to put a rainbow sticker on a machine gun,' declares poet CAConrad. If there's one thing homonormativity reveals, it's the troubling fact that *you can be victimized and in no way be radical; it* Leo *happens very often among homosexuals as with every* Bersani *other oppressed minority.*

This is not a devaluation of queerness. It is a reminder: if we want to do more than claw our way into repressive structures, we have our work cut out for us.

* * *

A student came to my office the other day and showed me an op-ed piece his mother had published in the *LA Times,* in which she describes her turbulent feelings about his transgender identity. 'I want to love the man my daughter has become,' the mother announces at the outset, 'but floundering in the torrent of her change and my resistance to it, I fear I'll never make it across my river of anger and sorrow.'

I talked with the student politely, then came home and raged, reading parts of the mother's op-ed aloud. 'A transgender child brings a parent face to face with death,' the mother laments. 'The daughter I had known and loved was gone; a stranger with facial hair and a deep voice had taken her place.' I couldn't tell what made me more upset – the terms with which the woman was talking about her child, or the fact that she had chosen to publish them in a major newspaper. I told you I was sick of stories in the mainstream media told by comfortably cisgendered folks – presumably 'us' – expressing grief over the transitions of others, presumably 'them.' ('Where does it fit into the taxonomy of life crises when one person's liberation is another's loss?' Molly Haskell asks in her anguished account of her brother's MTF transition. In case her question is not rhetorical, I'd suggest the following answer: pretty damn low.)

To my surprise, you did not share my outrage. Instead, you raised an eyebrow and reminded me that, just a few years ago, I had expressed related fears, albeit not articulated in exactly the same terms, about the unknown changes that might be wrought by hormones, by surgery. We were standing in our kitchen when you said this, at the same countertop where I suddenly remembered scouring the teeny print of a Canadian testosterone information pamphlet (Canada is light-years ahead of the United States on this front). I had indeed been trying to figure out, in a sort of teary panic, what about you might change on T, and what would not.

By the time I was scouring the pamphlet, we'd been trying to get pregnant, without success, for over a year. I stayed busy trying to puff up my uterine lining by downing gobs of foul-smelling beige capsules and slick brown pellets from an acupuncturist with 'a heavy hand', that is, one who left my legs covered with bruises; you had begun to lay the groundwork to have top surgery and start injecting T, which causes the uterus to shrivel. The surgery didn't worry me as much as the T – there's a certain clarity to excision that hormonal reconfiguration lacks – but part of me still wanted you to keep your chest the way it was. I wanted this for my sake, not yours (which meant it was a desire I would need to dispose of quickly). I also discovered that I harbored some unexamined butch bravado on your behalf, like – *You've had a beard for years and already pass 90 per cent of the time without T, which is more than many folks who want such things can say; isn't that enough?*

Unable to say such things, I focused on the risks of elevated cholesterol and threats to your cardiovascular system that T might cause. My father died of a heart attack at age forty, for no sensible reason (*'his heart exploded'*); what if I lost you the same way? You were both Geminis. I read the risks aloud ominously, as if, once revealed, they might scare you off T for good. Instead you shrugged, reminded me that T would not put you in a higher risk category than that of bio males not on T. I sputtered a few half-baked Buddhist precepts about the potential unwisdom of making external changes rather than focusing on internal transformation. What if, once you made these big external changes, you still felt just as ill at ease in your body, in the world? *As if I did not know that, in the field of gender, there is no charting where the external and the internal begin and end –*

Exasperated, you finally said, *You think I'm not worried too? Of course I'm worried. What I don't need is your worry on top of mine. I need your support.* I get it, give it.

As it turned out, my fears were unwarranted. Which isn't to say you haven't changed. But the biggest change of all has been a measure of peace. The peace is not total, but in the face of a suffocating anxiety, a measure of peace is no small thing. You do feel grief-stricken now, but only that you waited so long, that you had to suffer so acutely for three decades before finally finding some relief. Which is why each time I count the four rungs down on the blue ladder tattooed on your lower back, spread out the skin, push in the nearly two-inch-long needle, and plunge the golden, oily T into deep muscle mass, I feel certain I am delivering a gift.

And now, after living beside you all these years, and watching your wheel of a mind bring forth an art of pure wildness – as I labor grimly on these sentences, wondering all the while if prose is but the gravestone marking the forsaking of wildness (fidelity to sense-making, to assertion, to *argument*, however loose) – I'm no longer sure which of us is more at home in the world, which of us more free.

* * *

In response to a journalist who asked him to 'summarize himself in a nutshell,' John Cage once said, 'Get yourself out of whatever cage you find yourself in.' He knew his name was stuck to him, or he was stuck to it. Still, he urges out of it. The *Argo*'s parts may get replaced, but it's still called the *Argo*. We may become more used to jumping into flight, but that doesn't mean we have done with all perches. *We ought to say a feeling of and, a feeling of if, a feeling of but, and a feeling of by, quite as readily as we say a feeling of blue or a feeling of cold.* We ought to, but we don't – or at least, we don't quite as readily. But the more you do, the more quickly you can recognize the feeling when it comes around again, and hopefully you won't need to stare as long. _{William James}

* * *
* * *

Don't produce and don't reproduce, my friend said. But really there is no such thing as reproduction, only acts of production. No lack, only desiring machines. *Flying anuses, speeding vaginas, there is no castration.* When all the mythologies have been set aside, we can see that, children or no children, *the joke of evolution is that it is a teleology without a point, that we, like all animals, are a project that issues in nothing.* _{Andrew Solomon} _{Deleuze/ Guattari} _{Phillips/ Bersani}

But is there really such a thing as nothing, as nothingness? I don't know. I know we're still here, who knows for how long, ablaze with our care, its ongoing song.

ACKNOWLEDGEMENTS

For material included in this selection the following grateful acknowledgements are made: to Claudia Rankine for her poems from *Nothing in Nature is Private* (The Cleveland Poetry Center at Cleveland State University, 1994), *The End of the Alphabet* (Grove Press, 1998) and *Plot* (Grove Press, 2001); to Denise Riley for her poems from *Marxism for Infants* (Street Editions, 1977) and *Selected Poems* (Reality Street, 2000), as well as her poem 'All, as a rule, fall towards their wound'; to Pan Macmillan via PLSclear for poems by Denise Riley from *Say Something Back* (Picador, 2016); to Maggie Nelson for her poems from *Shiner* (Hanging Loose Press, 2001), *The Latest Winter* (Hanging Loose Press, 2003), *Jane: A Murder* (Soft Skull, 2005), *Something Bright, Then Holes* (Soft Skull, 2007); to Jonathan Cape for material by Maggie Nelson from *Bluets* (Wave Books, 2009; Jonathan Cape, 2017); and to Melville House UK for material by Maggie Nelson from *The Argonauts* (Graywolf Press, 2015; Melville House, 2016).

FURTHER NOTES ON DENISE RILEY'S POEMS

'Lure' uses the title of a 1963 Gillian Ayres painting. The poem adapts, misquotes, or rephrases song lyrics: 'The Great Pretender' written by Buck Ram, recorded by The Platters in 1955; 'The Wanderer' written by Ernie Maresca, released by Dion in 1961; 'It's In His Kiss' written by Rudy Clark, sung by Betty Everett in 1964; and the title of 'When Will I be Loved' written by Phil Everley, recorded by the Everly Brothers in 1960.

'A Misremembered Lyric' borrows a phrase from 'Rhythm of the Rain' written by John Gummoe, sung in 1962 by The Cascades; also a phrase adapted from 'Something's Gotten Hold of My Heart' by Roger Cook and Roger Greenaway, recorded by

Gene Pitney in 1967. The poem also quotes a couplet from a 1924 song by The Two Gilberts, cited by Graham Greene.

'Shantung' includes misquotations from Marvin Gaye's 1963 song 'Can I get A Witness' and from William Shakespeare's *Macbeth*.

'Poem Beginning With a Line From Proverbs' adapts Proverbs 27, verse 17, from the King James version of the Bible.

'Rayon' ends with a phrase by Chuck Berry from his song 'Carol', written and recorded in 1958.

'Well All Right' has a last line echoing the song 'Life' by Sly and The Family Stone, 1963.

'Oleanna' borrows the title of David Mamet's 1992 stage play.

'Dark Looks' has an italicized borrowing, as spoken by Jeanne Moreau, from the script of Bertrand Blier's 1974 film *Les Valseuses*. The poem also alludes to the 1953 film 'Niagara', starring Joseph Cotten and Marilyn Monroe.